# Places You Live

Printed in the United States of America

First Printing, 2017
ISBN 978-0-9974670-2-4
Editing and Design by Red Dress Press
Olympia, WA

For Lukus.

*Jeg elsker deg,*
*kjaere*

The author would like to thank the following:

Liz Shine * Christopher House * Emelita Trier * Nate Hile * Kenneth Hile * Lukus Walker * Darrell born * Grandma * Gloria Martin * Bryan Willis * Coffee * Iris Murdoch * Poets * Victor Hugo * Mary Shelley * Flannery O'Connor * Ludwig van Beethoven * Edvard Munch * Readers * Medusa * Neil Gaiman * A.S. Byatt * Frida Kahlo * Amiri Baraka * Amanda Palmer * Carson McCullers * Edward Albee * Truman Capote * Diane Wakoski * Edgar Allan Poe * Chuck Palahniuk * Grendel's Mother * Love * Jane Kenyon * Bob Dylan * Pablo Neruda * Catwoman * Vincent van Gogh * Margaret Atwood * Samuel Taylor Coleridge * Julia Margaret Cameron * Hel * Dorothy Allison * Charlotte Bronte * Zora Neale Hurston * Alice * Mark Twain * Jim Croce * E.E. Cummings * Sylvia Plath * Asbjornsen & Moe * Anne Sexton * Emily Dickinson * William Blake * Charles Dickens * My friends & family * William Shakespeare * Cindy Sherman * Gene Wolfe * Lewis Carroll * Atonal Intervals * Carl Jung * Moliere * Sigrid Undset * Elliott Smith * Oscar Wilde * Ani DiFranco * Mary Magdelene * Stephen Fry * D.H. Lawrence * Giacomo Puccini * Charles Rennie Mackintosh * Toy Cameras * Richard Browning * Toni Morrison * Cats * Albert Camus * John Steinbeck * Hugs * The Beatles * Red Dress Press * Marc Chagall * The Pacific Ocean * Denise Levertov * John William Waterhouse * Alphonse Mucha * Christina Rossetti * Jonathan Swift * Fairy Tales * Gabriel Garcia Marquez * Thomas Hardy * Emily Bronte * Stevie Nickes * Chaim Potok * Jacob & Wilhelm Grimm * Tidepools * Hans Christian Anderson * Anne Bradstreet *Odd Nerdrum * Octopi * The Huldra * Mikhail Bulgakov * Henry James * Leo Tolstoy * Kristy MacColl * Wassily Kandinsky * Marcel Proust * Merfolk * David Foster Wallace * Herman Melville * Pianos

# TABLE OF CONTENTS

# Places You Live

# Birth

Sweaty hair undulates
like a kelp forest
on the bleached white pillowcase.
From across the curtained room
vibrating waves of Tangled up in Blue
compete with the buzz
of fluorescent bulbs.

Somebody wearing
a top smothered in
rainbows pulls my legs,
white as ghost crabs,
farther apart.
Two voices
near the foot of the bed
discuss fetal heartbeat and
Fourth of July plans.
        Push!

I clench my teeth,
mouth tight as a cockle shell,
bear down,
watch the clock,
remind myself
to breathe through the burn.
        Push!
I vow to never--
        Push!
        Push!
        Push!--
do this again.

Someone nestles a
baby boy into my arms.
He nuzzles my breast.
I wonder if I could, supposing
I wanted to, do this
just one more time.

# Sixteen Candles

You colored me a picture
on the kids' menu at the burger joint and
twisted my hair around your finger and
gave me a cupcake with a blue candle;
it was just enough.
Then every time I called you
there were chores to do and
leaks to fix and
engines to rebuild;
I found contentment in
a bottle of wine and
a late showing of A Room with a View.

And I gave up on you.

Then you knocked on my bedroom window
at 2 o'clock in the morning hungry for manicotti;
I lit white candles and
pretended this was something
I knew how to do.
You made me read you my poems, out loud.
Every single one; You leaned in close;
My stomach a brick.

But it never happened; instead
you leaned back on the couch and
crossed your arms and
asked me why my poems
were so sad.

# Going to California

What is called galloping off,
jumping ship, running afoul of
your husband, is sometimes
only a refusal to grow up, a
stretching out of legs that never
asked to be bent up origami-style
on a bench too narrow
even for a child.

What is called selfish,
looking out for number one,
all wrapped up in oneself,
is sometimes only a self-
reconnaissance for the
possibility of rapture, like
eating a cold spoonful of
ice cream straight from
the carton, like swiping the
power company's money from
the kitty to buy a new pair of
panties made to cling to
magic hips, hips that never
asked to bear children.

What is called an omen,
a karmic harbinger, bad news,
is sometimes only a name
given, not chosen, an excuse to
shed sensible shoes and
kick your feet for freedom,
the hat in your hand
a Tin Lizzie wending west
toward a great open ocean.

# Blackberries

I beg you
pretty please
pick some
blackberries for me
because all the ripe ones
are the tasty ones
all the pretty ones
are up way too high
I just can't reach
I'll never be tall enough
even if I stand on your dictionary
on top of a metal bucket
on top of a lawn chair.

I'm thirsty
but I probably
wouldn't be if
I had some blackberries
and I wouldn't bother you
for lemonade
or iced tea
or even a glass of water
and I'd play outside
practically the entire day
and I wouldn't
interrupt you when
someone called from
far far away
just to talk to you
forever
about some
stupid wedding
and I mean forever
and I'll sleep in my
own bed the whole night
if you pick those berries for me

I'll even say thank you
and tell you
you're the best mom

I've ever known
maybe even in the whole state.

I'm hungry
and I couldn't
finish my cereal because
you brought it to me
right in the middle
of building the greatest fort ever
and by the time I was finished
the milk had made it all mushy
and I didn't eat my lunch
because there was this
teeny tiny black thing
on my sandwich
that looked like it might be
a piece of dirt
or a baby ant's leg
so I had to bury it
behind the hedge in the backyard
so the worms could eat it
because I cut a worm in half
I'm sorry
with dad's shovel last week
to see what worms
look like on the inside
I'm pretty sure worms
love peanut butter
and guess what
if I get some of those berries
I won't say
no matter what
that dinner looks like sheep brains
even if it's something disgusting
even if it's something I hate

even if it's tuna casserole.

I beg you
pretty please
with whipped cream

and chocolate sprinkles on top
and pistachios
because I know you like them
even though they're green and gross
and look like monster teeth
stop reading your silly book
put on your flip-flops
pick me some blackberries
I only want
I don't know
about one giant bowlful
because you really love me
when we come back inside
your fingers will be all purple and red
and if you say we have to
wash them and chill them
and save them for a pie
I will bite you
I won't be able to help it
I want my blackberries
warm and dirty and oozy.

## Stone

Everywhere I walk, shadows
cross the sidewalk like
carvings on headstones.
And here I thought there would
be no spaces unreachable by light.
Every day I cut across
some invisible line, commit
some faux pas, offend massive
stone angels, or stout mobs of
crows, or even the shroud of
white carnations lurking
in the cremation garden.
Everything I am trying to
say I have already said. It is
like bowing your head to
pray and then
forgetting how words work.
It is like scratching at
a stone only to
remember, red blood
ebbing under
your fingernails, that
it's still a stone.

14

## This Moment

I snip the sunburned leaves of arugula,
toss them into the steaming pile of rotting
cardboard, coffee grounds, crusty bread
too tough to eat, even toasted.

I think the dead are most alive in these
moments; my cats know this, they pace behind
the sliding glass door, warning with trills and
guttural growls. I see nothing, but I feel their
pull like a fat ache around the perimeter of
the garden bed.

I bow before each plant, apologize for
cutting off a limb in order to save the
the body, offering things half-alive to
buy more time, knowing all the while
what happens in this moment
happens all the time.

# Runaway

Even in shadow
Her eyes are full of color
Turquoise domes in Bukhara
Blue milk mushrooms
Coltrane on the turntable at midnight

Even under the starry night
Her eyes are a Subterranean home-
Sick kind of blue
Berry stains on faded jeans
Blue notes
Ridin' that midnite train

## Sticks and Stones

From the kitchen window
I watch him swing a wooden sword with
one hand; under his other arm he has
tucked a shoebox from a pair of
sandals I bought last summer.

The garden gate he used to be
able to barely peek over on
his tippy toes now stops mid-
chest. Two of my terracotta pots are
a mess of clay shards crushed with
a mighty blow some afternoon when
I was too busy with dinner or
too bewitched by a book to notice.

He lies down on his stomach in
the grass and opens the box; he touches
the treasures inside and complains to
himself before hopping up.
I'm so bored!

He opens a snot-colored book,
*Gross and Disgusting Science Facts* and
lies down on the couch. When
I look over, he has fallen asleep with
the sword and box beside him. I peek
inside: nothing but some sticks and
stones and a sticker I gave him inside
a birthday card three years ago that
says, I'm Proud of You! Way to Go!

# My Father Mows the Lawn

My father mows the lawn,
wipes sweat that flows
down his forehead with
the back of his hand, wipes
his nose and cheeks,
tarnished brown
of smoked salmon skin.

From the lake, a hundred bufflehead
ducks hear his roaring machine and
soar up into a vociferous pyramid of
brown smudges.

He would prefer to be
making soup, or painting a
model car, or reading a biography, not this
madness, this always running things over,
cutting them down,
scaring them away.

# Depression

The grass has not been mowed in weeks.
Houseflies hover over a bird
decomposing and half-buried in dandelions.
A once-turquoise Ford Country Squire station wagon that
your cousin was only going to leave here a month, two max, still
sits in the back yard, eleven years later, its headlights missing,
every window smashed out, the vinyl simulated wood trim
barely hanging on.
A shirtless boy on the sidewalk is
tying a skateboard to his bike with a nylon rope.
He screams at his younger brother to hurry up and
get on the skateboard or he is not going to give him a ride.
The air smells like lighter fluid, charred hot dogs,
and dandelions.
Every time the boy yells
the neighbor's Beagle barks and bays
from behind the chainlink fence.
How do you apologize for being tired of
being tired of everything?
A toad croaks.
It starts to drizzle.
Steam rises off the hot asphalt.
I breathe in the mineral smell and wish
I hadn't worn these shoes.
A load of dingy whites hang from
the clothesline like ghostly
post-it note reminders of my failures.

# One for Sorrow

When I am born
They shake a cup.
Cast down water, sky,
The hardest of rocks.
He presses these
Into the round softness of my skull.

Flycatchers perch on the picket fence
With bellies white as the petals of the daisies
He wraps around my wrists.

He can not hear music anymore
And grandma will not let him drink
So when he gets bored
He whisks me up into his arms
And waltzes me away.

I sneak into his bedroom
Help myself to nickels, bottlecaps, a tie clip
A pretty bird with shiny treasure.

Outside my window
Crows pick at the wheat
He moves my body side to side
Grunt-hums Alouette
Into the mattress.

The dark green of a dragonfly's tail
Shimmers in the sunlight
Like the spittle trails across my bruised shoulder.

Not the maker of the cup
Not the dragonfly
Not even you know how
He moves
The things he razes,
The things he begins to build.

One for sorrow.
Two for joy.

Three for a funeral.
Four for birth.
Five for heaven.
Six for hell.
Seven for the devil,
His own self.

## Crossing

Cornbread and milk.
Flowered aprons.
Baking soda baths to
soothe chicken pox.
Sleeping side-by-side on
the hide-a-bed.
If it hadn't snowed that
night, I never would
have learned to
make cinnamon rolls.

Why, oh why, didn't
I love you more?

Whether you
grieve simply or
with great force you
have to wade into
that rank river, drag yourself
through bodies, thick as
fiddlers in hell, on
your own two feet.

And if you should
wake again, if you should
return, you must drink from
the river where Shadow
and Darkness stand
guard, lonesome for
the likes of you.

Drink! Taste the
sweet nectar of
forgetfulness, love,
love the taste. Long
for it, but refuse to cross.
This is a toll you're
not ready to pay.

# Chrysanthemums

He tells me he loves me more than his hound
more than the picture of his mother tacked to the bedroom wall
more than the leaves when they change from green to brown
so I let him hold my hand

Bourbon whiskey and a helter-skelter chivalry
are his true hankerings
but he swears if I stop wearing so much pink
eat more red meat
open the curtains and let the sun shine in
he'll fill my cupped hands with pomegranate seeds
so I let him rest his head on my shoulder

He tells me he wants me more than his car
more than his friends
more than football
though preliminary probing proves
what I don't give willingly he's happy to steal,
but I let him kiss me

He tells me Happy Birthday
hands me chrysanthemums the color of dried blood
holds the palm of his hand against my abdomen
but this is not a season for beginning

# [hold my hand]

hold my hand through this narrow corridor
this jazzed-up war machine of a city
'cause we're too cool for
these hipster men in sweater vests
these wooden women
drinking white wine from stemless goblets
these people that
eat money
breathe money
sleep money

hold my hand down this dark alley
let's dance with smiles to match that fortune cat
waving from the greasy back window
let's discover
one step at a time
where this goes
what is implied
by your hand in my hand
delicate as a maple leaf

## If You Want Me

If you want me, traipse through
foxglove, spillover of
pale lavender & heavily
spotted. Go barefoot. Don some
saffron orange gloves. Show me
you mean it.
Outlove the blue
TV screen light. Live with
dirt under your fingernails. Roll in
the clover wearing last night's dress like
Friday's child. This lasts
just a little while.
If you want me, prepare for
disaster, un-loveliest boilover of
blood and bone. Affliction flickers in
me. In love is pain. In pain,
muscles stretch. You must understand
you understand nothing.

## Someone Will Kiss You

Someone will sit with you in
a rusty pick-up truck at
four in the morning and listen to
you ramble on about the
cold stare of a blank page.
Someone will turn your heart into
a letter box cluttered with movie stubs, little
paper fortunes from cookies delivered with the
bills at Chinese restaurants, and
letters written when two days—
two hours—was too long to be apart.
Someone will kiss you under
an apple tree that has grown up with
you in your parents' yard, and you will
open your eyes, stunned by the
simple star-shaped blossoms.

# Everything Flies Away

Her dress hangs
empty across the world.
A blue ribbon
ties one sleeve to
a park bench, the other
to a statue of an eagle.

Her dress flaps
in the wind; it makes
a sound like the combs of
a paper wasp's nest being
crushed by a canvas sneaker.

Her dress is
a tri-color flag,
evidence of
the two grave
accidents she
suffered in life:
one, being rich,
the other,
being poor.

Her dress flutters
over gas stations,
marble columns,
and wildfires.
It makes
the skyscrapers
wanting.

Her dress twitches;
it says: everything
flies away and
everything clings tight.

# Leitmotif

Before you can climb a tree
you must stand at the bottom.
Before we can come together
we must be disentangled.
Before my hand can nestle so perfectly in yours
it must live solitary as a spider.
Before thirst can be quenched
you must long for a drink.
Before you can eat
you must hunger and kill.
Before you can be satisfied
you must know disillusionment.
Before you can lay your head on the pillow and dream
you must suffer weariness.
Before you can heal
you must be broken.

## Coming Home

From the back porch she calls my name.
She stands under a bower of Marketmore cucumbers
In a pink dress covered with primroses.
The sky behind her is drab and mottled as old bone.

She stands under a bower of Marketmore cucumbers.
Sometimes I forget she is there until my skin prickles.
The sky behind her is drab and mottled as old bone.
Her neatly pinned hair still smells of moss and vanilla.

Sometimes I forget she's there until my skin prickles.
I am a girl on her knees in the dirt praying for you. To you?
Her neatly pinned hair still smells of moss and vanilla.
This dream only resembles a story of a grandmother coming home.

I am a girl on her knees in the dirt praying for you. To you?
Some things we know without knowing.
This dream only resembles a story of a grandmother coming home.
From the back porch she calls my name.

## Late Afternoon

So this was the dream: The garden is
weary, over-plump tomatoes hang from
the vine, the sky oxblood red.
I see you through the kitchen
window. You walk through
the grass toward the back porch.
You try all three lawn chairs,
but you choose mine,
because it is just right.
You wear a pink dress,
your hair freshly curled,
your feet bare, toenails
painted red.
I wash spinach leaves and
watch you twirl in the grass,
arms spread wide open.
I plunge the spinach leaves under
cold water again and again.
My fingers go numb.
Only one thought repeats:
Is it deranged to spend the afternoon
watching a dead woman dance?
I don't know. I dry the
spinach leaves and pull
open the drain. It sounds
like someone sobbing.

# Nochebuena

In a clash of brick and steel, time fractures:
one moment drinking hot chocolate in the courtyard
watching a girl with a poinsettia in her hair
teach a red-headed Amazon to whistle,
then the collapse,
my body, the piñata,
smashed pieces of clay
you pray can be put back together again,
fastened and fused.

These enormous wooden beads
and tiny embroidered shoes distract the eye,
but what lies beneath is still pale, still broken.
My skull and your photographs
are all that remain intact.

Someday someone who thinks himself clever
will say, "Aha, this is the day she thought about
dying!" But you'll know better, sitting in your
red velvet arm chair, legs crossed. You will know
this as the day I thought about life.

In the rosy candlelight of this last night
you swallow one more shot of tequila,
but nothing could be more normal than this:
you stumble beside my bed, bring the needle to
my arm, your hands smell of pork and masa,
already I am flying over the blue house,
flame leaf in my hair.

## Sunset

The sun glows,
the caudal fin of
a California Yellowtail.
Look how flawlessly
it infiltrates everything,
like a rumor in
the workplace.
Suggest...
Suggest...
Saturate.

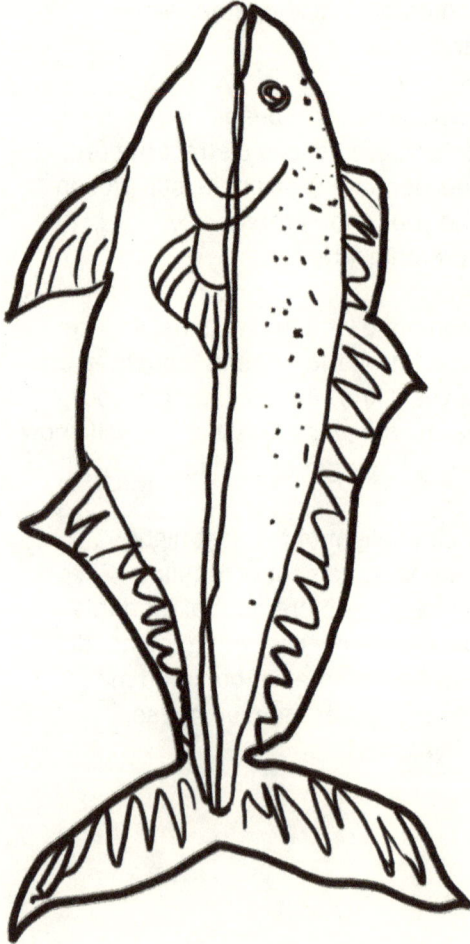

## At the Piano

My fingers root for the cold
keys, the slightly off-center
middle C, the hammer striking
steel, nineteen tons of tension string.
I play all night to garrote you.
I play until the sonata
palpitates, resonates, reverberates.
One bare foot poised over
the sustain pedal, one
foot flat on the floor, I make
these notes collide, grope, fuck.

One measure for every
time you tried to do me in.
Beethoven played with
such passion pianos would
fracture and shatter beneath
his hands. And how much
rougher you played on
your instrument.
Can a body
recover from
that kind of love?

Chords progress with
a palpable goal, each
accented beat blasting
your belly, your crotch, your
throat. But I still don't feel what
I wish I felt. Measure for
measure it is revealed this is
an imitation of Beethoven; this is
a masquerade of murder.

## Summer Light

Somewhere in Norway there is
a brook bountiful with brown trout.

"You can just reach right in and
grab them with your hands.
Table for two, please."
Brown trout with spots of
black and orange and red.
When I was young I thought they were
gods escaped from other worlds.
"Careful now,
they're slippery little devils."

\*\*\*

Summer light stipples the
kitchen floor where
she stands, still barefoot.
"Sometimes it seems like
she's only half there.
More often than not these days."
She slides the fillet knife down
along the backbone, not really
looking, humming a song he is
not familiar with.
"If you choose a bashful bride,
don't be surprised when
she's stiff and silent as the sea."

\*\*\*

He lights the candles on
the dinner table. She likes
the lights dim; he does not like
paying the electric bill.
"The blue anemones are
in bloom. Saw some on
my morning walk."
She smiles at some point past
his head and lifts the tumbler of

cold water to her lips.
He tears a piece of bread off
the loaf, butters it, hands it
across to her. As she reaches
to accept, sunlight from
the kitchen window blushes across the
pale skin of her forearm.
"Bit early for bikinis though."

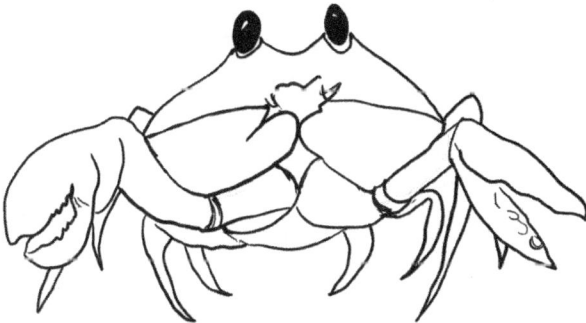

# Fireworks

If there are sparks
you know it is meant to be.
Fuel and an oxidizer bind
like summer lovers.
Get yourself someplace cozy and
prepare for blast off.
Indulge in that breathless moment
between lighting the fuse and explosion,
that moment when your stomach lurches and
you wonder if you truly can pull this off.
Get all caught up in the
bang and bloom of
pyrotechnic stars,
because this is life,
because the moon is no bigger than a fly's eye,
because tonight the legs of spiders--
red, blue, white--travel the sky.

# Fever

Snowflakes like
down feathers tumble onto
the frozen pond outside
my window, but my
cheeks burn.
I stick my tongue out &
cannot taste the chill. So,
there is a cold I cannot
catch! (Alas, I am not
cooped here for defence.)
O, Winter, if you could nip, or
sting, or close your arctic
fingers around my throat. Just
not this, not this
falling–so
close–without relief, with-
out frostbite, without numb.
Snowflakes flutter through
the air like the shavings of
fingernails, but I am stuck in
bed forced to remember one
thing; my body is married to fire.

## Eternity

I woke to find
not quite what
I had in mind:
a sharp shard of
glass in hand,
an angel
beside my bed,
feet aflame.

       Do not believe
       this will not hurt,
       that you will
       never be forgotten,
       that you will not
       wake up alone
       choking on
       shadows.

I've met
too many
demons to
be frightened by
the devil so
get the hell away
from me.

       I am not
       your devil and
       I am not
       your death.

I'm too
far down the
spiritual mover
chain to
warrant any
sort of
guardian angel,
that's for
damn sure.

38

I am not
your angel and
I am not
your savior.

Can you
save me?

Your feet always
take you where
you need to
go, though
they may
flinch at broken
glass forever.
What you look for
looks for you.

## On My Way Rejoicing

To go on my way rejoicing can be dangerous, like
writing a dadaist poem, like accepting a sandwich from
a man with the head of a goat. I mean, it's probably
safe to eat (right?), but goats (like some men) tend
to browse with their tongues. I open my mouth like
a well-loved cookbook & take a bite.

To go on my way rejoicing requires some silence, but
my stillness makes the goat man uncomfortable. He
coughs and yawns and fidgets to fill up the quiet of
what he calls my sullenness. The goat man says that
wherever two or more are gathered together there
is the potential for one hell of a party.

To go on my way rejoicing is to love, but
love is a key and keys are hard to find and
sometimes the locks change. The goat man says
that love is not a key. Love is a feather. He says it
is also a fire. He licks my lower lip, bites gently, sucks like
mad. I think what the goat man is trying to tell me is that
love is a temple between the feather and the fire.

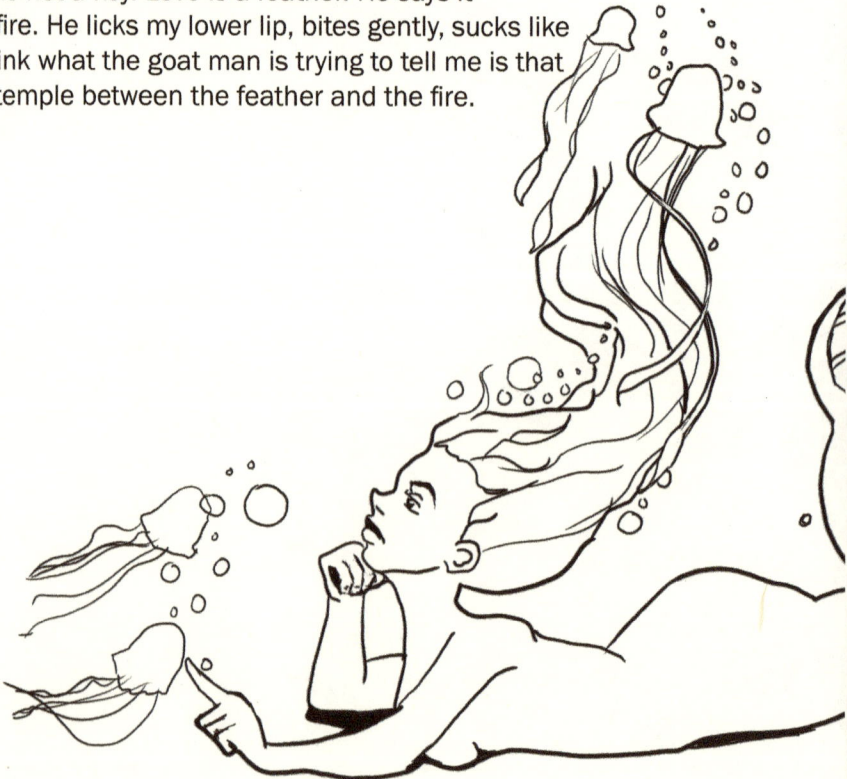

## Desire

All she has to do is
loosen that buckle &
all thought unravels.
There may be
urgent paperwork scattered
in front of me. I may be
holding a blue ball point pen
mid-signature.
She bends her
knee &
reaches down.
Nothing else matters.
One foot in front of the
other & one day at a time are
words people say when
they do not know
how to float.
Desire is begotten
sextillion different ways:
the first movement of
the Moonlight Sonata, honey spread
across hot bread, the unbuckling of
a sandal strap.

# [because you are so often alone]

because you are so often alone
i would like to hold your hand in
the courtyard of the blue house
shoot the breeze
cradle your stubbly head
(i never loved you for your hair)
in my hands after you've had
too much tequila

because you are so often alone
i would like to bring you home
feed you oysters and geoduck
light your cigarettes
walk the trails among the waterfalls
(your tiny feet flicker like doves)
dance in the fountain
wearing Tehuana dresses

because you are so often alone
i would like to paint your lips red
crown you with roses
run my fingers over your brow
plant a tree of hope in your heart
(my star of the sea)
no need for knives to prove my passion
our revolution begins with a kiss

## The Goatherd

Sometimes he will let them nibble on
bushes with bright red berries. He is
indulgent, often for no reason the goats can
discern. The men call him fool when
he walks by. The women are certain these
berries are why his goats are so happy.
One day he reaches out and
plucks some berries for himself. He keeps
them in a pouch around his waist. When
it is dark, and the goats are
sleeping, he makes a wish and
throws the berries into the fire.
He rakes the beans from
the hot embers, grinds them, stirs
the gritty grains into his hot
water. He inhales, takes a sip. Sometimes
it tastes so good, he sets the cup down and
dances around the fire like a goat.

# Places you Live

a russet leaf
refusing to let go

words written to
someone I can't
remember

a girl's body slipping free
from a shivering ash

weather worn rocks

cypresses bathed in fog

the last question
you get to ask

a pacific redwood so
colossal we could never
reach around it

a lit flame

the water of tears

a howling river
steadfast in pursuit of
the gaping abyss

# Kenning

The whale road wobbles the wave steed,
billow maiden after billow maiden frothing
at the mouth, the tree man opens his
arms for the sleep of the sword.
There are no breakers of rings on the wave steed,
no thralls, only the billow maidens, and
the sky's jewel screaming from the
mouth in Ymir's skull, and the tree man in
the wave steed hungry for the sleep of the sword.
The tree man in the wave steed cares not where
the whale road carries him, as long as it is near
the weather of weapons, or the sleep of the sword,
or both. The tree man is a feeder of ravens;
there is mind's worth in spear din.

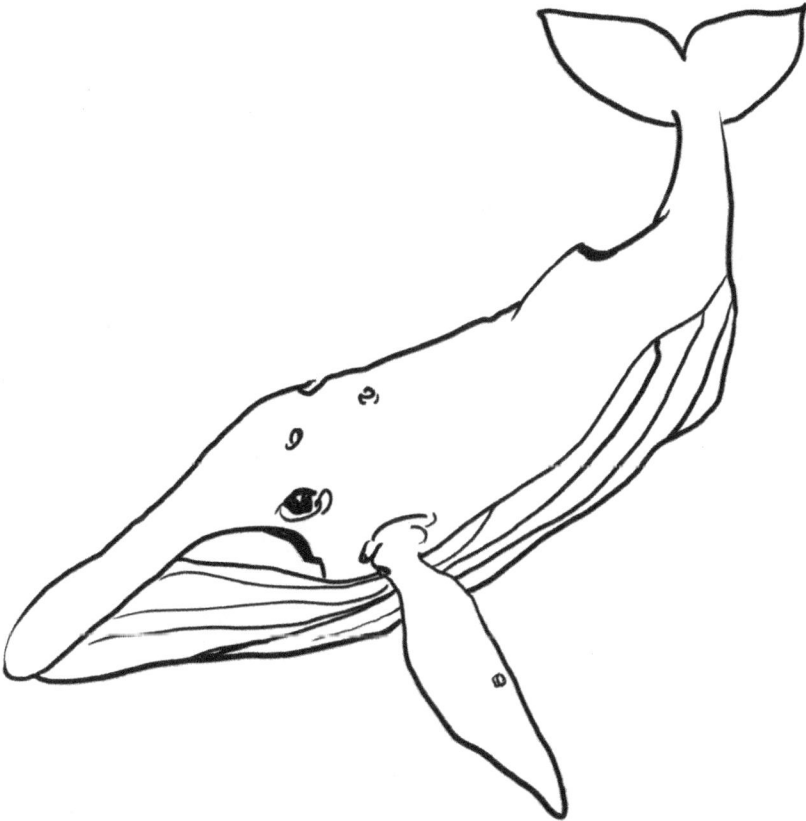

## The Rain Here

The first time it rains I am
a wreck. I have been
warned, listened to stories of
basements filling slowly with
water, animals floating by
vacant family room windows, the
neighbor rowing to work.
I imagine my baby being
whisked away, cradle and
all, down Barnacle Street, lift him
carefully into my arms, with
great ceremony, like I might never
get to do it again.
I run upstairs and attempt to
pack a bag, a stupid
plastic grocery bag, with
all our necessities.
What is necessary?
I've never lived in
a city that flooded.
Not like this.
Never.
The rain in this new place, this
windblown city I've been
moved to, the rain here is
scornful. It assails
mothers carrying groceries through
supermarket parking lots.
It crushes flowers, and has been
known to steal umbrellas right
out of tightly clutched fists. The
rain here hops in
the driver's seat, takes
a joyride, and never looks back.

# Fisherman's Knot

He sits in the grass near the edge of
his dinghy, head bent over, and attaches
the line to the sharply curved hook.
This is the first knot he learned to tie, from
watching our uncle do it a million times one
summer. Back when the fish actually bit.

He remembers his
uncle's head bent over,
the purposeful look, the
nimbleness of
his scarred fingers.
He would say,
If a knot ever fails you,
ninety-nine times out of
one hundred it'll
be 'cause you done
something wrong.

He wets the loops with some spit.
With tag end and standing end in
one hand, the bend of the hook in
the other, he tightens the knot–
unwavering and unhurried.

He reaches into the pocket of
his stained overalls and pulls out
a cigarette, lights it, takes a slow drag.
He touches the hot cigarette to
the tip of the tag end, creating
a perfect ball.
He is meticulous about the
details of this ceremony and
will not tolerate any
interruption from me,
like each knot is sacred,
like each knot might be
the knot that saves his life,
like each knot is a poem.

## Swell

I fell in love with
a surfer boy. Does
it feel good? If not, it
isn't surfing.

Your body and
a board and
a wave.

Who would wish for
tennis shoes and
dirt trails when
you can glide
across the ocean?

\*\*\*

I fell in love with
a surfer boy,
salt on
his lips, his
shoulders like two
russeted apples, the
way he'd tilt his
head and
say, *swell*.

He stamped my
hand with the
letters L. O. V. E. He is
serious enough not
to write the declaration in
magic marker, which is
never truly
permanent. The
molecular gears and
levers of the skin always

chanting: rejuvenate,
rejuvenate, rejuvenate.

He didn't dare
go so far as
a tattoo because
everything comes to
an end before
beginning again, the
cyclic mass of
love being no
exception, but
still I wore those
four letters as
my heart's opus on
my opisthenar.

I could feel the
vibrations swell and
dilate in my veins, the
tension of the
pressure flow, the
heated desire of
diffusion drawing love
into the cells.

\*\*\*

I fell in love with
A surfer boy, imagined
love was something
scattered. I had simply to
spread my fingers and
the seeds would
disperse, seeds that knew
when to make an entrance, where to
hunker down, where to thrive.

Those four letters remind me
some things can be
salvaged and some should be
left to glide.
L.O.V.E.
Does it feel good?
Let it go.

# Of the Waves
## (for Kenneth)

A little boy stands on
a box in too-big
blue jeans, munching on
carrot sticks that
become microphones.
His ten fingers and
ten toes are
twenty gulls that
say, *Good luck*
*slowing us down!*
I rush through
school days, dinners, banged-up
knees, birthdays, barely
pausing to bend down and
breathe in the sweet and salty.
He stands barefoot on
a cardboard box and
plucks at a guitar, build
a ladder to the stars and
climb on every rung.
Sometimes I forget that
this boy who swells and
breaks like every breath is
everything, this boy who
knows a clock different from
the one hanging on
our kitchen wall. This
boy's laughter could
slake a hungry sea.

## Conversation

I was too afraid to get too close.
I remember my mouth moving,
Words whispered on the white hospital blanket,
Him saying between breaths,
*Speak!* Breathe.
*Up!* Breathe.
*Damn!* Breathe.
*It!* Breathe.
I wanted to lean in a little closer;
I wanted him to hear what
I needed to say.

I opened and closed
My fists like jellyfish,
Like after the closing
Must surely come the opening,
Like if I opened and closed and
Closed and opened enough times
I might propel myself into the air and
Across the room to the potted purple orchid beside
The soap dispenser, its labellum a polka-dot
pocket full of words never heard.

## Lunch

When I was small, I would
take my grandfather lunch and
watch the brewery workers dressed
in their blue overalls and thick-
soled boots, open wax paper-
wrapped sandwiches and
cold bottles of beer. They would
eat and laugh and stretch their
long legs out beside
the lunchroom tables.

I imagined they were
happy men because I only
saw them at lunchtime, steel
lunch boxes swinging open, sharing
weekend gossip. I didn't know that
after the whistle blew they went
home to tension that could
take a man's hand off, the taste of
bitterness so strong no beer could
wash it away.

## Budd Bay

She leans over
the landing and drops
pebbles into Budd Bay.
Smooth rocks work
their way out of
her hands into
the murky water.
The afternoon sun tints
everything pale yellow-brown, like
Polaroids from the 1970s. Her hair,
tucked behind a pierced ear, spills
between the slats of boardwalk, strands
brush her forearm. Protein filaments.
She drops another pebble.
Plop.
The surface shivers.
On a bench further down
the wharf an old man clips shades onto
his eye glasses. A woman with incredibly
curly red hair sits down next to him and puts
a blanket across his knees. The woman shouts at
the man, "Sit up straight!"
Water lit by late summer sun.
Surface tension.
Ripples, whose shape time cannot hold.

## Brother

Barely born before they set in motion stories about you
thundering forth from thighs of clay, stories of your hair
shining finer than gold even through the mask of
waxy white vernix, stories of your perfect posterior,
too precious to be transported in anything less than a chariot.

With fat fingers you pull at the ships on strings
hung above your cradle. Cooing and content
you tug a red mainsail, then a blue, drawing closer
with every fistful to the father of the sea-thread,
bubbles rise from your plump lips.

But they tell other stories, stories about
the sinkhole of my mouth, a cauldron that calls
my brother to storm his vessel into the very eye of my soul,
which is the gallows of the gods. When the story
reaches you, you close your eyes and hold your breath so long
they fear you might die right then and there--
your death driving destruction.

In the beginning they separated us, banished me beneath
the roots of the wind-rocked tree where I peer up into
the pattern of your prison, pierce the woven webs of
your waves. My blue words hunt for you in whispers of fate,
whispers of waiting, whispers of the promise we made
to sip the silver water until blood blooms and
blossoms in this world between my mouth and yours.

# Blue Door

A blue door is
after all
just a door whether
it opens into
a cluttered
downtown alley or
into the glory of
the Beloved.
Her t-shirt says
Oly Girl but
she's never spent
the night on
a beach so
we lock the
front door and
trip toward
the coast because
you aren't awake until
you've been roused
by waves.
On the door of
the bathroom stall
someone has written
*Do unto those*
*downstream as*
*you would have*
*those upstream*
*do unto you!*
in permanent
royal blue.
She drinks too
much wine and
falls asleep between
poems so I stoke
the fire and walk
for the waves,

the walk a passage,
an artery bursting,
an undertow into
the blue door of the sea.

# All Things are Made from Water

You wore yellow boots in
the rain, but no hat. You said
you liked the way the water
felt running down your face.

But I dove in. Headfirst.

I miss the sound your
bare feet make when
you would walk across
the bedroom floor.

My feet splashed as

I followed you under like
a billion bitsy glass
beads bumping against
each other.

Did I leave you lonely?

I took sanctuary on the
bank of the Deschutes:
salmon, my guitar & a
cold bottle of beer.
I screamed at the
fish all night.

What else did I miss?

A house full of dogs, a
little girl with violets in
her hair, so many songs.

Violets! Oh.
Oh, Love, how
did I get to this place?

You dove in. Headfirst.
You didn't say goodbye.

The pain, Love, the pain.
The pain pricked and
gashed. Its many
reds darkened and
crusted and outpoured again.

So you ended it?

I wanted to
dive under with
an uncontrollable
greed.

Did I really want
more than I needed?
Tell me why
you needed the water.

The only thing that is
truly mine is this
body, my body.
(Mine!)

I was made from
water, to water I returned;
I dove in headfirst, every
scar on my body swept smooth.

# What The Rain Washes Away

A woman sits on
the edge of the road in
a blue pinstripe dress and
shakes her head from
side to side, God-damned
consumer culture, she says and
washes her feet in a bucket of
rainwater and I don't know if
she's weeping or it's
just the rain.
Things are consumed, says
a man standing outside what
used to be a charming dive of
a cafe & tobacco shop but is
now some upscale chain eatery.
*That's just the way it is*! he says, but
he says it like he does not
believe it, he says it like
He is talking about
his mother who has
recently passed away.

A couple in matching
green jackets hold
hands as they rush
down the sidewalk,
patchouli and coffee in their
wake, they push their
shoulders against
one another as if
keeping any rain drops from
falling between them can
keep the rain from
washing everything away.
The mud puddles teem with
beat up stalks of

mint, a canary yellow
condom, empty clove
cigarette boxes, a seagull

feather, and a
pink plastic barrette.

## Apology

Back when you
asked me if I was sorry—
you, wearing a red striped
t-shirt, barefoot at the river, those
bold brown eyes, you only wanted to
make paper boats and a better sister out of me—
When I said no and bit my lower lip hard to keep
from crying, still you knew, somehow; you nodded,
the smallest of nods, and breathed air in quick through
your front teeth, and then you just let it all go with
one look, and gave me a bear hug anyway—
Please forgive me. I get stuck in places like
a bad wind up toy, I take round and happy
and make it windswept and mangled—
Sometimes I have no tongue, just
a rock, heavy and pink, choking
up the waterway.

# Emerald City

I am at the clock tower on
New Year's Eve watching
the half-silvered sphere of
the moon voyage east.

I watch the moon, bury
my hands further in my
pockets, breathe slow so
this does not feel so much
like the end of something.

I breathe in the ghost fog of
the people of the lakes, breathe in
the woodchips and turpentine of
a great fire, breathe in the
endless cups of coffee.

I breathe even as the
skeleton tolls his bell, breathe
because the universe is
a theatre, a theatre that circles
a small golden star, a circle that
summons a midnight moon.

# Jormungandr

The serpent circles the earth
Swallows its tail
Separates earth from sky
Splits all visible direction into two sections
Those that intersect the earth's surface
And those that do not

The serpent swallows its tail
So there is no beginning no end
So wherever you are there the serpent is also
Not as a threat but as a reminder
If you lose the serpent you lose the horizon
If you lose the horizon you lose the course

The serpent separates earth from sky
Sets apart that space in which our bodies reside
From that where our minds wander
It slips between worlds like a middle child
Sometimes the faithful friend
Sometimes the slayer

The serpent splits all visible direction
Into two sections
Squeezing the borderline
Between sight and perception
Between control and
The illusion of control

# Illness

She sits up slowly,
scoots to the edge of
the bed wearing
nothing but
a gauze bandage,
a reminder she is indeed mortal.
Her hair ripples brown, and
red, and silver.
She wears it down, either because
she thinks you prefer it that way, or
because she uses it as
a curtain beneath which
she flows,
head bent forward,
chin tucked,
bobbing like a bottle
caught in the current.
You raise her arms and
pull the blue dress over
her head. Leaning down
you lift her hair like
a veil, and kiss
her pallid cheek, the
smell of her skin so
far from pain, so
far from the dosing of
pills. You are in lavender
up to your knees–tentative, but
past the need for guarantees.

# Court

Sitting on gnarl-knuckled hands, my
grandmother watches her sister play
tennis every weekday afternoon during
the summer of nineteen seventy-three, knowing
trouble does not stick to everybody, it bounces off some
people like a little yellow ball.
My grandmother is a happy woman despite
trouble, despite rarely being in on the joke, despite
her sister's golden Best Female Player trophy.
Sometimes life serves one perfect tennis ball after
another. Some people are born with a racquet in their
hand. Some people just smile while one ball hits them, then
another, and another, too embarrassed by their
ugly arms to lift them up and
shield themselves from harm.

# Willow

He has a hacky sack, balloons for
blowing up and filling with
water, a magnificent walking stick he
found by the lake at grandpa's house, but
he stands on the front steps, hands in
his pockets, watching the wind blow the
leaves on the willow tree.

Two fearless robins touch down before
flying away in opposite directions, dandelion
seeds scatter, the kid across
the street hollers over and asks if
he wants to play baseball:
no such luck.

He sighs and steps inside, pulls off
his dad's huge cowboy boots, tilts
his head to one side, asks if
he has to take a bath tonight and
if so why does he have to take
a bath tonight and do I know the
tree in the front yard doesn't ever
take baths and yet she has
beautiful green hair?

# Dreams

Someone dreams of a heaven like
a bonfire where ragged hand-me-
downs are torched and birth
certificates burnt to dust,
a heaven for bodies that
run twice as hard but never
reach the runner's high,
a heaven for hearts that
love and long but only get
bombarded and blistered,
a heaven for minds that
wend and leap but
barely manage to get by,
a heaven for those who
do not have the guts to be
a sinner nor the fortitude to be a saint,
a heaven where there are
no big sisters, no progress reports,
no such thing as a tag-a-long,
no trading knowledge for shame,
a heaven where you can
laugh as loud as you want, run naked in
the sunshine, host Easter egg
hunts every single Sunday,
a heaven where you can
poke your finger in the blue frosting of
a birthday cake and not get
sent to your room,
a heaven where it's perfectly
acceptable to love the smooth wrap and
curling bow of a gift as much as
the surprise inside, more than
who has the most and how much
did it cost,
a heaven with
no secret clubs and

no off limits,
a heaven where music is
dancing and singing together not

a brother rocking back and forth with
headphones on telling you to
shut up and go away,
a heaven where funny is
a virtue, where there is room for
silliness in your Sunday crossword puzzle,
inside jokes within your pencil drawings of
eyes and hands, romping room for
clowns in your precious leather-bound
masterpieces of English literature,
a heaven where there is
no reaching, no more
strain, just a falling back into
a lake of cobalt with
silver stars in your eyes—
enough.

# Runner

You are not
something I lose
like a key,
like my dignity,
like a phone number
written in pencil
on a cocktail napkin.

You are not
predictable
like a moth to flame,
not quiet
like the sun
plunging below
the horizon,
not vespertine
like witches' weeds,
not shrouded
like the seed nestled
in the yellow flesh
of a peach.

You dance
and sing,
your vibrato
so close that
my lungs fill
with your breath
when I sing.

You vanish,
oh, how you disappear,
how artful you are
at dodging.

You fade like
a cloak of fog,

head for the hills
like a girl's laughter,

split like the pod
of a scarlet runner bean,
tumble like the seeds
falling into the wooden pail.

You love
swimming holes,
fried okra,
white cotton nightgowns,
and no matter who might
need you around,
you love to run.

# Unfinished Letter

I try to write you a letter.
Each stroke claws
the delicate paper,
picks up bits of fiber,
tears. Ink bleeds.

I wish you had not
sat beside me on
the piano bench--
just to listen, steeped
a pot of tea, folded your
hands around that chipped
white mug and waited--
so patiently--for me to
let my guard down.

I wish we had not
lain on a red blanket
in your backyard--
our breath smelling of
oranges and bergamot--
and talked about
the stars like they were
exploding silver pearls,
our hands holding each
other's so tight we
could have become a
chip of ice on the
shadows of our moon.
I try to write you a letter.
My fingers itch with the enterprise.
The chair holds
the small of my back so
perfectly I am sure it is
your hand; I reach behind
me but touch only
spindles of wood.

I wish I could
walk away, burn

it down, forget
everything. Anything
but ending up beside
the piano, sipping
tea from a chipped
white mug, waiting
for it to speak to me.

# Dust

I have a confession to make.

I don't dust.
Not really.
Okay, not ever.
Well, sometimes it happens.
Accidentally.
Taking a novel off the bookshelf.
Rearranging furniture.
Reaching for the old blue teapot on top of the refrigerator.

You always said
the path to righteousness is
paved with slightly damp, lint-free cloths.
Dust ye: for the kingdom of heaven shines like
a fresh coat of furniture polish.

I want to dust.
No, really, I do.
Just not as much as I want to read Ulysses.
Or find a spider in the shower.
Or miss the last bus home.

# Blues

He suggests a walk, points out
the fresh green of spring grass, the new
leaves on the maple trees, grabs a fistful of
grass and sprinkles it over
my head and shoulders.
To be happy is to remember the
feeling that comes after; the
red balloon all blown up, buoyant,
will eventually pop, deflated on
the carpet, a pathetic, stretched-out heap.

He waves at me from
across at the lawn, smiles like
the summer sun. The smell of
blue barbecue smoke fills my nose.
I wave back and crunch on
my celery stalk. His hands are
so strong. Look how
at ease he is in his body.

He keeps all my letters in
a drawer with his neckties.
He kisses me with
his eyes wide open.
He could be happy but
my sadness makes him otherwise.

# The Fortune Teller

Her gnarled hands struggle to
Turn the patterned cards.
I want to reach across the table,
Flip them over for her,
Be the administrator of my own fate.
Instead, I hide my hands
Between the bottom of my thighs
And the tacky wooden stool.

The fortune teller says
"You will die many deaths
Before you die."
I try to welcome it.
With resolution and without remorse,
I let death touch my left shoulder,
Bow to the numbness that comes
With keeping at a distance,
Showing up but never taking part.

There is a story, a song,
In these scars creeping up my arm
Like silver-red crabapple branches
Drawing near the sun.

Sweet little baby,
I don't know where you've been.
Gonna love you baby,
Here I come again.

And he does come again.
And I do love him again.
And I love him again.
And love him again.

And when death pulls away,
As all lovers will,

I bite the flesh from my thumbs
Until red swims in
The tidepools of my fingerprints.

I chew the bits of skin like bubblegum.
The taste of blood like the taste of pennies
The taste of pennies like the taste of blood.

She speaks of deaths like stones that stack,
Stones that shape themselves into structures,
Stones that see into the spheres that
Share sanctuary with the dead.
Stones that know there is no difference
Between the red of the crabapple and
The red of her tongue and the red of
these branching scars.

# Maybe Next Time

Maybe next time
I won't spill over
like a shaker of salt.

Maybe next time
I'll shake the habit
like a red-lettered
single-serving packet:
Tear Here.

Maybe next time
I'll buy oblivion on credit,
dilly dally at the kitchen table
with my lime & tequila.
When it rains, it pours.

Maybe next time
I'll crash-land into the fire,
raise a ruckus to invoke the gods.

Setting a salt sacrifice in motion
hallows the world.

Maybe next time
I'll clutch the white pillar of my neck,
scratch below the surface,
let it flow.

After the excavation,
a crystalline shower.

# Lines

A sugar-stirring spoon
Red suspenders
An electric circuit loop
The point spread
A grocery list
Cocaine
Steel rails running on wooden ties
A cat's tail
Kohl powder penciled under bloodshot eyes
A simian crease
Point A to point B
The tone arm of a phonograph
Untied shoelaces
College ruled notebook paper
A football field
Crisscross sundress straps
Pink satin ribbons
A picture frame painted gold
Postcards from a childhood penpal
Walls
A filmstrip
The string attached to a tea bag
A sunflower stem
The end of a marathon
Veins returning blood back to the heart
A coloring book
Drought-dry earth
Van Gogh's dashed brushstrokes
Crow's Fcct
Daedalus' Labyrinth
Cirrus Radiatus clouds
A fading face drawn on the bathroom mirror

# Nine Short Poems About Stairs

If stairs led only
to good places, not dark
attics and government offices and
hospital rooms, more people might climb them.

Descending a spiral
staircase still scares me silly,
especially if it leads to a basement.

If you'd rather take the
stairs next time we visit the
doctor, I'm okay with that, but
maybe we should invite the stairs to
rise and fall with us a bit more frequently.

If I ever fall down the
stairs, please don't make a
scene. Let me stand up and
pretend like nothing happened.
And do not--ever--ask me if I'm okay.
Of course I'm not okay; I just fell down a flight of stairs.

There are days I feel
like an abandoned slinky that's
stuck in the shag carpet covering the stairs.
Unable to move up or down, I just shiver underfoot.

If I were tiny--
like a ballerina--I would
have a floating staircase that
leads to a secret chamber full of tutus.

As you slide
down the banister
of life, may you never
forget about the newel post.

Sometimes stairs remind
me of my mother on chore day.
One more thing. Did you clean your room?
One more thing. Did you put away the bath towels?
One more thing. Did you remember to dust the family room?

If I ever
ask you to
do just one more
thing more than once,
throw me down the stairs.

www.ingramcontent.com/pod-product-compliance
Lightning Source LLC
LaVergne TN
LVHW011412080426
835511LV00005B/492